D0310744

A CELEBRATION OF CHRISTMAS

A CELEBRATION OF CHRISTMAS

Caroline Harrington

St Michael

Editor: Donna Wood
Art Editor: Ursula Dawson
Designer: Hazel Edington
Picture Research: Liz Fowler
Production: Claire Kane

This edition first published in 1989
exclusively for Marks and Spencer p.l.c.
by arrangements with
the Octopus Publishing Group
Michelin House, 81 Fulham Road
London SW3 6RB
© Hennerwood Publications Limited, 1989
ISBN 0 86273 542 4
Printed in Great Britain by BPCC Paulton Books Limited

Contents

Introduction

OF
CHRISTMAS PAST

Christmas is a time of merriment and feasting, a time for indulging in all the traditional pleasures; the Christmas tree, presents from Santa Claus, turkey and plum pudding, cards and carols. Yet at the time Queen Victoria succeeded to the throne, none of these things was traditional at all. In fact for a great many people, the 25th of December was just an ordinary working day. The newspapers were published as usual, and rarely bothered to mention that this was the anniversary of the birth of Jesus Christ. Celebrating Christmas was a custom that had fallen into neglect.

ABOVE: Victorians were nostalgic for the Christmas spirit and largesse of times past.

But people could remember, or at least had heard about, the good old days, when Christmas really was Christmas. They were nostalgic for those merry, jovial times when everyone from the lord of the manor to the humblest servant joined together in revelry, as in this 1859 recollection of *Christmas in the Olden Times*:

> *Time was when the frost was on the pane, and snow lay thick upon the ground, when all the chimneys smoked and all the ovens were full . . . when all were full of gladness and both serf and squire, baron and retainer, did their very best to keep their companions happy. All classes gave themselves up to frolic and revelry, with a thoroughness of spirit.*

It was inevitable that such nostalgia would lead eventually to a revival of Christmas festivities, and that new life would be breathed into the old traditions.

There had been midwinter festivals since long before Christian times. The gods had to be propitiated during the bleak days of winter in order to ensure the return of the life-giving sun. For the Romans it was the Saturnalia, celebrated with evergreen decorations, the exchange of presents, and a great deal of drinking. In Northern Europe they called it Yuletide, and it featured feasting and wassailing around the Yule log fire. When the Christian church took over the midwinter festival to celebrate the birth of Christ, and declared that the whole of the twelve days between the Nativity and Epiphany should be a sacred and festive season, many of the pagan customs were adopted. At the courts and manor houses a 'Lord of Misrule' was appointed, and by Tudor times, in spite of the Church's admonitions, Christmas was being celebrated in a positive orgy of feasting, dancing, gambling and drunkenness.

Such conspicuous jollity was of course anathema to the Puritans, and when Oliver Cromwell seized power, they attempted to abolish Christmas; one of those misguided attempts (like prohibition in 1920s America) to legislate against people having fun. It was proclaimed that Christmas day should be kept as a fast and a penance, and for a dozen years any sort of festivity was banned. Parliament sat on Christmas day, its soldiers made sure that the shops stayed open, and the churches closed. Decking the halls with boughs of holly was taboo, and it was definitely not the season to be jolly. Understandably this gave a boost to the Royalist cause.

The Restoration in 1660 ensured that the laws against Christmas were repealed, but the old ways of celebrating Christmas had taken a knock from which they never really recovered. Also society was beginning to change quite dramatically. People who for generations had worked on the land began to move to the great industrial cities. They left behind the country house, the

BELOW: The Lord of Misrule, master of the revels in Elizabethan times.

farm and the village, and the seasonal customs associated with them. The country estates were bought up by new money, '. . . *the manufacturing and mercantile aristocracy who have no family customs to keep up, . . . planters from the West Indies, and adventurers from the East who have no feeling connected with times and seasons which they have so long ceased to observe'*. So Christmas revelry became for most people just a fond memory.

Charles Dickens identified this general mood of nostalgia for Christmas past, and set about recreating it

A CAROL FOR A WASSAIL BOWL.

in his writing. Christmas at Dingley Dell, as described in *The Pickwick Papers*, had nothing to do with real life in the 1830s; it was a thoroughly romanticized version of the festivities at an English country house in days gone by. But it was what people wanted and the images of this mythical 'Merrie England' still adorn our Christmas cards today: jovial squires dispensing good cheer by roaring fires, and coaches bowling along snow-covered lanes.

Modern Victorian Britain was a stark contrast to this cosy imagined past. While the country's new-found industrial prosperity brought affluence and leisure to lots of people, it brought terrible hardship to many more. The rich could not really enjoy the fruits of their prosperity without experiencing anxiety and guilt about the deprivations of those less fortunate. Charitable works and benevolence to the poor were the duty of the pious Victorian, all the more so during the season of goodwill, as *Punch* enjoined its readers in 1843:

> *What have you done this 'merry Christmas' for the happiness of those about you, below you? Nothing?*
> *Do you dare, with those sirloin cheeks and that port-wine nose, to answer – Nothing?*

In the same year, Dickens published *A Christmas Carol*. Gone is the unallayed jollity of Pickwick's Christmas, and in its place are the worthy philanthropic sentiments so graphically illustrated in the tale of Scrooge and Bob Crachit. Poor crippled Tiny Tim moved the sentimental hearts of the nation, and *A Christmas Carol* was an instant and popular success. By the end of 1844 15,000 copies had been sold, and that year no less than nine London theatres staged dramatised versions of the tale.

LEFT: Carol singers were rewarded for their efforts with the wassail bowl.

ABOVE: The lady of the manor delivers a Christmas hamper.

FAR LEFT: In Tudor times revelry continued until Twelfth Night.

The Wassail Bowl.

George Bernard Shaw commented acidly that the book was 'an exploitation of pre-existent sentiment of the vulgar Christmas kind'. But he had to admit that what Dickens had written was the perfect parable of the charitable aspirations of well-to-do Victorians.

Even the Poor Law Board, not generally associated with public-spirited generosity, were moved by the spirit of the times and gave permission for extra food to be provided in the workhouse on Christmas day, and a few years later even allowed female paupers 'a modicum of tea and sugar wherewith to regale themselves during the afternoon'.

'Perhaps the greatest characteristic of Christmas day at present', wrote William Henry Husk in 1868, 'is the very general custom of regarding it as a domestic and family festival'. Most people today, if asked what they thought about Christmas, would say, 'Well, it's really for the children, isn't it?' And this perhaps was the most significant change that the Victorians made in the seasonal celebrations. From being a social occasion where friends, neighbours, whole communities would get together in general revelry, Christmas became centred on hearth and home.

For Queen Victoria and her beloved Albert, it was very much a family occasion, a time when they could put aside affairs of state, and have fun with their children. The royal family was pictured in *The Illustrated London News* happily grouped around their Christmas tree, and naturally became a role model for every family in the land. Thus Christmas became, in a way that no previous holiday had, a time for indulgence towards the little ones, a festival most especially for the pleasure and enjoyment of children.

So the Victorians breathed new life into Christmas. They transformed a half-forgotten festival into a great family jamboree, a time for surrounding oneself with one's nearest and dearest, a time for goodwill and generosity, particularly towards children, and, of course, a time for Christian charity and benevolence to the poor. And to this resurrected feast-day they brought new customs, and established a tradition of Christmas celebrations that has lasted to this day.

FAR LEFT: A Christmas calendar, published in Punch *in 1843.*

LEFT: Three young carol singers carry the wassail bowl.

ABOVE: Children clamour to decorate the house on Christmas Eve.

Chapter One

THE
CHRISTMAS TREE

*I*t is commonly believed that Queen Victoria's husband, Prince Albert, introduced the Christmas tree into this country, bringing the custom with him from his native Germany. In fact it had been part of the festivities for many immigrant German families long before Prince Albert's day, and Queen Charlotte, the wife of George III, is reputed to have set up a Christmas tree at Windsor as early as 1789. But the custom didn't capture the imagination of the public at large until Victoria and her husband gave it the royal seal of approval.

The Christmas tree was of course a particular source of delight to the children. In 1841 Queen Victoria wrote of her own tree at Windsor:

'Today I have two children of my own to give presents to, who, they know not why, are full of happy wonder at the German Christmas tree and its radiant candles.'

In 1848 the *Illustrated London News* carried a charming portrait of the royal family, with by now five children, grouped around a twinkling fir. Victoria's subjects adored the royal family and aspired to make their own home lives as like as possible to that of their dear queen, and so it isn't surprising that the Christmas tree rapidly became the focus of the seasonal celebrations.

The anonymous author of a booklet entitled *The Christmas Tree* forecast its brilliant future:

'It now seems likely to become a naturalized plant. It is capable of adaptation to our national habits; and in less than a quarter of a century it will probably be familiar to all lovers of domestic observances, from the straits of Dover, to the Giant's Causeway, and John o'Groat's House; and even find its way to the wilds of Canada, and the banks of the Missouri and Columbia rivers.'

Indeed as the century progressed the fashion for Christmas trees swept across Europe and America. When in 1854 a giant spruce took pride of place at the Crystal Palace, it was clear that the Christmas tree had become accepted as a thoroughly British tradition.

Quite where its origin is to be found is a bit of a mystery. It has been suggested that the Christmas tree was a descendant of the Paradise Tree, or Tree of Life, as it was represented in many medieval plays about Adam and Eve. Or its roots may lie in the pagan winter

festivals, in which evergreens were used in fertility rites to ensure the coming of spring. But there is no record of decorated fir trees until about 1520, in Alsace, and by 1605 the tradition was already established in Germany, where '. . . they set up fir trees in the parlours in Strasbourg and hang on them roses cut out of many-coloured papers, apples, wafers, gold foil, sweets, etc.'

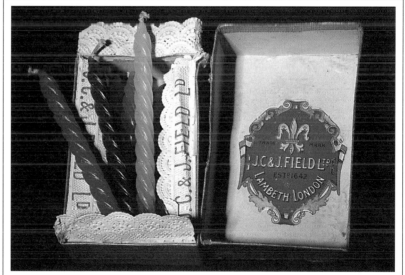

FAR LEFT: Victoria and Albert with their children gathered around the royal Christmas tree.

ABOVE: Candles produced for the Victorian tree.

LEFT: The giant Christmas tree at Crystal Palace, 1854.

The lighted candles which gave the Victorian tree its particular romantic appeal appeared later in the seventeenth century, although legend has it in Germany that Martin Luther was the first to decorate a tree in this way. The story goes that he carried home a fir tree and illuminated it with candles to remind children of the starlit heavens from which Jesus Christ descended so long ago.

In Britain, both lights and evergreens had long since been associated with the season and were regarded as part of the old 'Merrie England' Christmas tradition, so their happy conjunction in the Christmas tree assured its popularity.

Of course lighting a tree with candles had the disadvantage that they burned down very quickly, so the Victorian tree tended to be an 'occasion' in itself; it did not stand twinkling in the front parlour window for a fortnight, as our modern trees do. And to this day it is traditional in Germany to decorate the tree in secret and only reveal it to the children in all its glory on Christmas Eve. So it was in Victorian times; the tree was adorned, the candles lit, and only then was the family or party guests summoned to admire it. The other obvious disadvantage was of course that candles constituted a fire hazard. In Victorian times more fires were caused by candles than by anything else (particularly, so we are

ABOVE: Martin Luther's sixteenth-century Christmas tree, as visualized in the Illustrated London News.

RIGHT: Hoisting the Union Jack by Alfred Hunt from the Illustrated London News, 1876.

told, when people used them to look under the bed for burglars or chamber pots!). Party time was particularly hazardous, with girls in muslin dresses with their hair hanging loose, and cautionary tales abound. Under the headline *Fatally Burnt In Christmas Costumes* we read that '. . . fifteen children were set on fire, eleven of them fatally'. In grand houses a footman would be employed to patrol the tree, armed with a wet sponge on the end of a long pole, to douse the candles as they burned down close to the branches.

It was also recommended that gelatine lights be used, rather than candles. These were like night-lights, each one contained in a little cup of coloured gelatine, but since they had to be suspended below the branches rather than clipped to the top, there would still be a considerable danger of conflagration!

The risk of fire was overcome by the arrival of electricity, and the first electric fairy lights became available in the 1890s (though they remained a luxury available only to the well-to-do until well into this century).

After the illuminations have been secured in place it is suggested that '. . . a number of flags are requisite to add to the gaiety of the tree, which a few bows of coloured ribbon will also enhance.' *The Illustrated London News* in 1876 carried on its front page a picture entitled *Hoisting The Union Jack*, showing a little child being lifted up to

affix the flag to the top of the tree. Even then, however, it was more common to see a fairy perching on the topmost branch, thought to have been derived from the Christkind figure of German tradition, an angelic child who was reputed to be the bringer of gifts, a forerunner of Santa Claus.

As well as the flags and the ribbons, illustrations show that every inch of every branch of a Victorian Christmas tree was decorated with some gift or bauble. Although specially made glass balls started to appear as the century progressed, most Victorian tree decorations were hand made. Every year *Cassell's Family Magazine* came up with suggestions on how to make your own Christmas tree decorations and presents. Thus, cardboard was cut into stars, moons, leaves, swans, or any

LEFT: Happy Christmas, *by Viggo Johansen.*

ABOVE: Christmas at Windsor Castle, *1848.*

RIGHT: 'There was everything and more': toys galore for turn-of-the-century children.

other fancied shape, then covered with scarlet or gold paper and edged with remnants of lace; tissue paper was fashioned into paper roses and scraps of silk or ribbon sewn into tiny bags containing sugar plums.

By far the greatest proportion of Victorian tree decorations were in fact small gifts or sweetmeats wrapped with exquisite care and ingenuity, and one suspects that the tree must have looked rather bare after they had all been distributed. But beforehand it was a thing of boundless promise and enchantment. Here is Dickens' description of one such tree, in *Household Words*:

> *It was brilliantly lighted by a multitude of little tapers; and everywhere sparkled and glittered with bright objects. There were rosy cheeked dolls hiding behind the green leaves; and there were real watches (with moveable hands at least, and an endless capacity for being wound up) dangling from innumerable twigs; there were French-polished tables, chairs, bedsteads, wardrobes, eight-day clocks, and various other articles of domestic furniture (wonderfully made, in tin, at Wolverhampton), perched among the boughs, as if in preparation for some fairy housekeeping; there were . . . witches standing in enchanted rings of pasteboard, to tell fortunes; there were tetotums, humming tops, needlecases, pen-wipers, smelling-bottles, conversation cards, bouquet-holders; real fruit, made artificially dazzling with gold leaf; imitation apples, pears and walnuts, crammed with surprises; in short, as a pretty child, before me, delightfully whispered to another pretty child, her bosom friend, "There was everything, and more".*

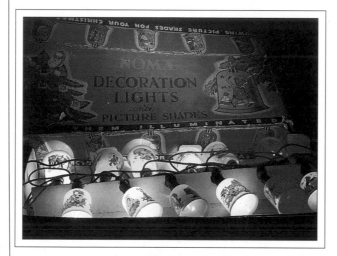

Most of the gifts Dickens mentions are the kind of thing we would put in stockings, though nowadays we would probably substitute bubble bath for smelling salts! But to decorate one's tree with tiny gifts for guests who drop in, or for a children's party, or just for family surprises, adds enormously to its charm.

The simplest container for sweets or nuts is a cone made of card. 'Be sure,' we are advised in *Cassell's Family Magazine* 'to join it so that there is not a hole in the point'. Then cut strips of red and green paper and paste them spirally at intervals, edge it with gold, and attach a loop of braid or gold thread to hang it from a branch. Another favourite kind of decorative container was a little drum made of cardboard (we can cheat by using a section from a toilet roll tube), again decorated with coloured paper and scraps of braid to look just like the splendid drums of a military band.

The Victorians delighted in disguising a present as something else, for example '. . . a soft pair of kid gloves can be rolled up, and secured in a large Spanish walnut shell previously emptied, and the two halves gummed together again' suggests *Little Folks* magazine. They must have been extremely fine kid gloves!

Many Christmas tree decorations were of course edible themselves; indeed the old German tradition was to decorate the tree almost exclusively with gilded nuts, fruit and gingerbread. *Weinachtskuchen*, exquisite little cakes and biscuits, like petits fours, are still enjoyed by German families at Christmas. Pretty biscuits to hang on the tree can be made by cutting a simple gingerbread mix into different shapes (stars, moons, bells, holly leaves, etc.). Make a hole with a skewer at the top of each one, bake, and then decorate them with coloured icing, silver balls, glacé cherries, hundreds and thousands. They can then be suspended on the tree by a piece

together. When it commences to candy, add one teaspoonful of lemon juice. Boil it quickly till it again begins to candy, butter a dish and pour the mixture quickly over it. As it cools cut it into thin strips, and twist it in the form of sticks.

Sticky sweetmeats, like sugar plums and marrons glacées, individually wrapped in silver foil, and hung on a piece of ribbon, can take the place of glass balls. The only problem is that the gilded fruit, the nuts and the sweetmeats were supposed to be left on the tree until Twelfth Night, when they would be consumed as the final treat of the Christmas season. It is difficult to believe that they would last so long.

of ribbon or cord passed through the hole.

Barley sugar twists make wonderful edible baubles, hanging like icicles from the branches and catching the light as they turn; here is a contemporary recipe:

Take twelve ounces of loaf sugar, a quarter of a pint of water, and half the white of one egg. Boil all

Chapter Two

CHRISTMAS
DECORATIONS

*E*vergreens have always been regarded as symbols of life continuing through the long cold days of winter. So they were used as decorations in pagan festivals, and the Romans, for whom evergreens signified good fortune, would deck their homes with holly and ivy and give sprigs of them to friends as good luck tokens during the mid-winter feast of Saturnalia. With the arrival of Christianity in Roman Britain, St Augustine was advised by Pope Gregory to encourage such of the local customs as were capable of Christian interpretation.

however, was completely beyond the pale, because it played a particularly significant role in Druid rites. The Arch Druid was supposed to have cut the mistletoe with a golden sickle and it was caught as it fell from the tree by virgins holding out a white cloth. There followed the sacrifice of white oxen, thought to have replaced human sacrifice, and the mistletoe was then divided up amongst the people, who took it home to hang over their doors to protect against witchcraft, and to ensure fertility. So at Christmas we may sing of the holly and the ivy, but never of the mistletoe, and to this day it is never used in church decorations.

But for decorating their houses at Christmas time, the Victorians used every kind of greenery they could lay their hands on. Gathering sufficient foliage was quite a task, and there would often be a family expedition to the woods. Enterprising countrymen would load up carts with evergreen branches, which they would then sell on the city streets. Holly, ivy, rosemary, bay, laurel, box, yew were all pressed into service, and used with the same abandon with which today we use paper chains or streamers.

Cassell's Family Magazine was full of good advice on how to decorate each room in the best possible taste. Evergreen chains, it suggested, could be made by sewing laurel leaves on to tapes or strips of calico, each leaf

It was easy for the Christian church to endow holly with the symbolism of Christ's crown of thorns. Ivy was a bit more difficult for them to adopt. It was the badge of Bacchus, the Roman god of wine. Mistletoe,

LEFT: A gift of evergreens delivered to the door deserved some reward.

RIGHT: Ropes of evergreens were used like paper chains.

BELOW: A ride on the holly cart.

being stitched on separately, 'a task which will furnish a few pleasant evenings' work to the younger members of the family'! These strips would then be used to decorate the hall, covering the walls from top to bottom in a criss-cross formation to create a lattice-work, with a cluster of holly berries fixed at each intersection. The effect must have been fairly overpowering, and defoliated quite a few laurel bushes!

Alternatively, you could make evergreen ropes, to hang as we would hang paper chains from each corner of the room to the centre.

Such ropes were also wound around the bannisters, and then a motto of welcome was fixed to the wall

facing the front door, or in as conspicuous a place as possible. A board, covered with red fabric or paper and edged with holly or laurel leaves, and adorned with a suitable text would greet your guests as they arrived. 'A Merry Christmas' or 'Season's Greetings' would suffice, but occasionally whole verses of poetry would grace the hall. A great deal of artistry went into these placards; sometimes the lettering was got up to look like ivory by spreading it with gum and sprinkling on raw rice or tapioca. Or it might be made to look like coral by painting the rice or tapioca pink (they used red sealing wax dissolved in spirits of wine); in this case the letters would naturally appear on a white background.

Holly might also be made to look snow-laden, by putting a little gum on the surface and sprinkling it with flour from a dredger, and if it was a bit short of berries, supplemented with dried peas painted red.

Archways and doorways were not to be left unadorned; a central rosette of leaves and holly 'intermixed if you like with some of the many coloured and white grasses and Cape flowers now to be had, and of an exquisite feathery appearance' would be placed at the top of the door frame. Smaller rosettes at each side would be linked to the central one by a festoon of leaves again stitched on to a calico base.

Similar quantities of evergreens were also considered

With fun and frolic
may you fill each day full,
And, kitten-like,
be always bright and
playful.

A Joyous time

appropriate for the decoration of 'dining-rooms, billiard rooms and corridors', but a less cumbersome and heavy style was thought more becoming for drawing rooms and boudoirs, where it was sufficient simply to twine sprigs of holly around the edges of picture frames and mirrors. Even bedrooms could benefit from a little festive treatment. Indeed in some country areas, in a

LEFT: Decorating the church in 1876.

ABOVE: Chinese lanterns, sometimes used amongst the evergreens.

RIGHT: Still life of Christmas Roses by Charles Etienne Gustave; fresh flowers add elegance to the decorations.

vestige of pagan superstition, decorating the bedroom was believed to ward off bad luck, as *The Lady* reported in 1893: *'. . . our West Country girls have a pretty custom of trimming their beds with holly on Christmas Eve. They say evil spirits will harm them if they omit this . . . ceremony.'*

Such an abundance of evergreens could produce a rather sombre effect, so coloured glass balls or Chinese lanterns might be introduced amongst the greenery. And 'the general effect is heightened and the decoration becomes more elaborate and more elegant' by arrangements of fresh flowers, such as chrysanthemums, Christmas roses, stephanotis, primulas or camellias.

Mistletoe may have had slightly sinister Druidic associations, but no Christmas was thought complete without it, and the maiden who escaped being kissed beneath it at Christmas time, it was said, had no hope of marrying within the year. It was therefore suspended in the most unavoidable place, usually from the central chandelier in the hall, or as Dickens describes in *The Pickwick Papers* from the kitchen ceiling:

> *. . . old Wardle had just suspended with his own hands a huge branch of mistletoe, and this same branch of mistletoe instantaneously gave rise to a scene of general and most delightful struggling and confusion. . . . Mr. Winkle kissed the young lady with the black eyes, and Mr. Snodgrass kissed*

ABOVE: Gathering mistletoe was a serious business.

RIGHT: Seizing the Opportunity, from Graphic Supplement, 1887.

FAR RIGHT: Mr Pickwick steals a kiss at a Christmas party.

*Emily; and Mr. Weller, not being particular about
the form of being under the mistletoe, kissed Emma
and the other female servants, just as he caught them.*

In an age hide-bound by propriety, the opportunity afforded by mistletoe, to kiss and embrace people out of wedlock, out of one's own social class, and even for women to approach men, was not to be missed, and then as now mistletoe was used as an excuse to plant kisses where they were least expected. In *The Diary of A Nobody* Mr Pooter is very perturbed when his decorous suggestion that enemies should kiss and make up is taken further than he intended:

was about to do, he kissed Carrie and the rest of the ladies. Fortunately the matter was treated as a joke, and we all laughed; but it was a most dangerous experiment, and I felt very uneasy for a moment as to the result. I subsequently referred to the matter to Carrie, but she said: 'Oh, he's not much more than a boy.' I said that he had a very large moustache for a boy. Carrie replied: 'I didn't say he was not a nice boy.'

Mistletoe was not always just hung in a bunch; some-

. . . a young fellow named Moss, who was a stranger to me, and who had scarcely spoken a word through dinner, jumped up suddenly with a sprig of mistletoe, and exclaimed: "Hulloh! I don't see why I shouldn't be in on this scene.' Before one could realise what he

times it was fashioned into a kissing ring. Two circles of crinoline cane were used (we can use two wire coat-hangers bent into circles), fixed at right angles to each other to form a sphere. Then mistletoe, mixed with other greenery was tightly bound with twine to each spoke of the sphere. Sometimes fir cones would be mixed in, and even rosy apples suspended from it, which formed part of an older tradition, the Advent Wreath. The latter had been the centrepiece of Christmas celebrations before the Christmas tree gained pride of place.

The Advent Wreath had four candles, one of which was lit for every Sunday in Advent, set in a horizontal ring of evergreens and fir cones, suspended by ribbons from the ceiling. A variation of this was used as a wonderful centrepiece for the Christmas dinner table, with any number of candles set into the ring and the ribbons tied in bows between them. Another suggestion was to cover an inverted basin with moss and stick lots of sprigs of holly into the moss to form a pyramid. On the top should be perched a figure of Old Father Christmas 'which may be bought in any bazaar or sugar-plum shop'.

By 1896 however, we find *The Lady* reproving its readers for being 'content with a few stiff, tastelessly arranged sprigs of evergreens', and suggesting:

LEFT: A pop-up Nativity scene from the 1880s.

BELOW: An elegant centrepiece is an important part of the festive table.

FAR LEFT. Painting Nativity figures, 1898.

'. . . a decidedly novel notion for the adornment of a Christmas dinner or supper table. Down the centre of the table runs a long narrow strip of looking glass, bordered all round with a bank of feathery moss, holly, mistletoe and sprays of red-veined tree ivy, in which . . . some fairy lights are half hid. At each *corner a miniature Christmas tree . . . gleaming with frostine powder, is fixed. The mimic lake is studded with islands of greenery, from which rise other little trees, and here and there are placed birch-bark canoes, painted with silver paint, and each apparently guided by a 'Father Christmas', bright with silvery drapery, the boats being freighted with glittering white bon-bons. The effect of the whole is striking and quaint.'*

No Christmas table would be without crack-ers, which were invented in the 1840s by a London

LEFT: Smartly dressed children pulling a cracker, 1878.

RIGHT: A festive cracker catalogue from 1925.

ABOVE: A selection of Tom Smith's colourful crackers from the 1900s.

pastry cook named Tom Smith. While on a trip to Paris, he admired the French custom of wrapping bonbons in a twist of coloured paper, and imported the idea into Britain. In an effort to stimulate sales he experimented with putting a love message into the wrapper, and marketing them as 'Kiss Mottos'. The idea did not really catch on, until one day, sitting by the fire, observing the logs spitting and crackling in the hearth, he hit on the idea of putting in the bang.

According to the *Strand Magazine* Tom Smith's company regularly produced crackers that were three feet long, containing a full-sized coat, hat, collar, frill, whiskers, umbrella, and eyeglass. But the biggest of all was made for the clown Harry Payne to pull every night at the pantomime at Drury Lane. It was seven feet long and contained a change of costume for Harry and his fellow cracker-puller, and a multitude of ordinary sized crackers, which were thrown among the audience.

Modern crackers can be hugely disappointing, so it is a good idea to make one's own. It is possible to purchase the 'snaps' ready-made from a joke or magic shop. All the other requisites – paper, card, glue, trimmings (and patience!) – are easily available, but if the prospect of making crackers is too daunting, buy some very cheap ones, and opening them carefully, exchange the contents for something appropriate to each person (and

don't forget to put the person's name on the outside). You can also add some extra decoration, and even think up jokes that will amuse each individual to replace the rather bland riddles that tend to come in cheaper commercial crackers.

Chapter Three

PARTY TIME

For a generation which set such store by modesty and propriety, it is astonishing the enthusiasm with which Victorian grown-ups would join in the most physical and boisterous of games at their family parties. They obviously believed that Christmas was a time for letting one's hair down. Perhaps this was a remnant of the old law, which in the reign of Henry VIII had expressly forbidden the playing of games 'under pain of twenty shillings to be forfeit' at any time *except* Christmas. Imagine how much steam was let off in *those* circumstances!

'A Christmas family party! We know of nothing in nature more delightful!', wrote Dickens. *Cassell's Family Magazine* was a little more circumspect:

> *'Unfortunately, family parties do not inevitably mean concord, though they ought to do so . . . Everybody can, at all events, endeavour to bring goodwill and a*

smiling countenance. . . . This is peculiarly the children's time, and we would have them as happy as we were in the old Christmas Days of long ago.'

Today's children watch an average of nine hours television on Christmas day. The Victorians had far more imaginative ways of filling the hours, and Christmas for them was undoubtedly party time. The grown-ups would have soirées, balls and other entertainments of their own, but the real fun revolved around the children, even the most venerable could enjoy a game of 'Hunt The Slipper', as the writer known as 'Uncle Tom' recounted in the *Illustrated London News*:

> *'It is not a little amusing to note the struggle with pride that sometimes assumes a place upon the countenance of middle-aged and old people when they are pressed into the service of 'Hunt the Slipper', and how at last the solemn man of business, and the staid matron, yield to the solicitations and the example of the lighter-hearted folk around them and, with comic gravity, sit down on the floor and play their part in the game. A grave sergeant-at-law, or the elderly author of an incomparable and incomprehensible treatise upon metaphysics, or a spectacled physician of sixty sitting on his hams on the carpet, and passing the slipper under them with all the dexterity, if not the glee, of a school boy, is a sight to be enjoyed.'*

Many games were particularly associated with this season of the year. A dramatic but rather hazardous occupation called 'Snapdragon' was one such: raisins were placed into a shallow dish and brandy poured over them. Then the lights were turned out and the brandy set on fire. The participants would take it in turns to try and snatch the fruit from the flames, to the accompaniment of an old rhyme:

> Here he comes with flaming bowl,
> Don't he meanto take his toll,
> Snip! Snap! Dragon!
> Take care you don't take too much,
> Be not greedy in your clutch,
> Snip! Snap! Dragon!
>
> With his blue and lapping tonge
> Many of you will be stung
> Snip! Snap! Dragon!
> For he snaps at all that comes,
> Snatching at his feast of plums,
> Snip! Snap! Dragon!

The lurid glare from the burning brandy lighting up the faces of the players was recommended as having 'quite a weird-like effect'. An even more hazardous version, called 'Flapdragon', was played in the West of England. A lighted candle was floated in a dish on the top of a can

Christmas Eve.

LEFT: Street urchins attracted by Sounds of Revelry in Augustus E. Mulready's 1886 painting.

ABOVE: The dangerous game of Snapdragon, illustrated by Eddie J. Andrews.

of ale or cider, and the task of the game was to drink the liquor without extinguishing the candle. 'This,' according to the instructions, 'is not done without the face being either blackened or slightly burnt'.

Another game was 'Hot Cockles': one person would be blindfolded and kneel down with his head in someone else's lap and his hand behind him, palm upwards. He would then call out 'Hot cockles, hot!', whereupon the other players in turn would hit his hand, and he would have to guess who had hit him. It was a game not without hazards, as demonstrated by this seventeenth-century letter to the *Spectator* magazine:

> *I am a footman in a great family and am in love with the housemaid. We were all at hot cockles last night in the hall these holidays, when I lay down and was blinded, when she pulled off her shoe and hit me such a rap as almost broke my head to pieces. Pray, sir, was this love or spite?*

Many of the games traditional to the Victorians are still played today, such as 'Hide and Seek', 'Hunt the Slipper', 'Musical Chairs', 'Simon Says' and 'Blind Man's Buff'. Here is the party at Scrooge's nephew's house:

> *'. . . There was first a game of blind-man's buff. Of course there was. And I no more believe Topper was really blind than I believe he had eyes in his boots. . . . The way he went after that plump sister*

ABOVE: A game of Blind Man's Buff, illustrated by W. St. Clair Simmons.

RIGHT: Eager anticipation as Father Christmas makes a welcome appearance at a children's party.

FAR RIGHT: The Queen of Sheba, a variation of Blind Man's Buff for adults.

in the lace tucker, was an outrage on the credulity of human nature. Knocking down the fire-irons, tumbling over the chairs, bumping against the piano, smothering himself among the curtains, wherever she went, there went he! He always knew where the plump sister was. He wouldn't catch anybody else. . . . She cried out that it wasn't fair; and it really was not. But . . . at last, he caught her; when, in spite of all her silken rustlings, and her rapid flutterings past him, he got her into a corner whence there was no escape . . .

A charming (and somewhat more decorous) variation on 'Blind Man's Buff' was known as 'Shadow Buff'. A white sheet or tablecloth is hung up to form a screen and a bright light shone on to it. The 'blind man' sits on the dark side of the sheet, and has to guess the identity of the other players as they pass in front of the light, casting their shadows on to the sheet. Disguises are allowed: funny hats and false noses, even a cloak draped Dracula-fashion to form the shadow of a bat. If the 'blind man' cheats and peeps he has to pay a forfeit; otherwise anyone correctly identified has to take his place.

'Chinese Whispers' is well known as a game where a message whispered from person to person gets gradually garbled. The Victorians enjoyed a different game of bad communications, which was called 'Russian Scandal'. Someone would write a short story, making it as full of wild intrigue as possible. The author would then take one other person out of the room, and read the story aloud to him, once only. The second person would then relate the story, as well as he could remember it, to a third, the third to a fourth, and so on until each member of the company had heard the story. The last person would then tell the story, as he heard it, to the full company, and then the original would be read out. 'It is quite curious,' comments *Cassell's Family Magazine* ingenuously, 'to notice how it has altered in

Mr. Fezziwig's Ball.

the course of transmission'.

Adults were not averse to joining in the rough and tumble of games like 'Musical Chairs', but they doubtless preferred the more sedate amusement of word games like 'The Minister's Cat', where everyone has to

FAR LEFT: Mr Fezziwig's Ball from A Christmas Carol.

LEFT. Adults were not too dignified to join in the fun and games at a Victorian Christmas party.

think of an adjective to describe the minister's pussy, beginning with A and working through the alphabet ('The Minister's cat is an angry cat, a boring cat, a cantankerous cat,' etc.). Then there were memory games, like the one which Kipling immortalized as 'Kim's Game' (attempting to remember twenty objects displayed on a tray), or guessing games; 'Twenty Questions' was a favourite long before it became popular on the radio. It was sometimes known as 'Charac-ters' or 'Nouns', or 'Yes and No'.

Scrooge's nephew and his party also played a general knowledge game called 'How, When and Where' – so Trivial Pursuit is not such a new invention after all!

Acting or miming games were tremendously popular; one such we now know as 'Adverbs' or 'In the Manner of the Word'. One player is sent out of the room, while the others decide on an adverb ('haughtily', 'clumsily', 'merrily'). When the first player re-enters he

rhymes with the chosen word, and then Team One has to devise a mime of what they think the chosen word might be. An incorrect mime is greeted with hisses, a correct one with applause and anyone resorting to speech has to pay a forfeit.

The one game no party could possibly be without was 'Charades'. The Victorians preferred the team version, and it really is much more fun when the people involved are not very good at mime. Each team chooses a word and devises a little scene for each syllable, eg. 'belfry' (bell/free), 'mosquito' (moss/key/toe), hospital (horse/pit/all), and then a final scene illustrating the whole word.

The Victorians loved practical jokes, like sending somebody off to hunt for something that was actually pinned to his back. In *The Diary Of A Nobody*, Mr Pooter is thoroughly discomfited by a joker out to subvert his decorous enjoyment of an evening's games:

We went over to Cummings' in the evening, and as it was cold, we stayed in and played games; Gowing, as usual, overstepping the mark. He suggested we should play "Cutlets", a game we never heard of. He sat on a chair, and asked Carrie to sit on his lap, an invitation which Carrie rightly declined.

After some species of wrangling, I sat on Gowing's knees and Carrie sat on the edge of mine. Lupin sat

challenges other individuals to perform an action or mime (walk, drink a cup of tea, put on a pair of gloves) 'in the manner of the word', which he has to guess.

In 'Dumb Crambo' the company is divided into two teams; Team One leaves the room, while Team Two thinks of a word. They tell Team One a word which

A LONG TIME AGO.

on the edge of Carrie's lap, then Cummings on Lupin's, and Mrs. Cummings on her husband's. We looked very ridiculous, and laughed a good deal.

Gowing then said: "Are you a believer in the Great Mogul?" We had to answer all together: "Yes – oh, yes!" (three times). Gowing said: "So am I," and suddenly got up. The result of this stupid joke was that we all fell on the ground, and poor Carrie banged her head against a corner of the fender.

After the party games, the jokes, the laughter and the falling about, it would be time for everyone to sit

LEFT: Mr Pooter and friends play at 'Cutlets' in an illustration from The Diary of a Nobody.

ABOVE: A Long Time Ago . . . storytelling by the fire.

RIGHT: The storyteller's audience is spellbound.

quietly while individual members of the company entertained with their 'party pieces' – singing a song, playing the piano or the harp, reciting a poem, or perhaps doing some conjuring tricks. And then there would be ghost stories; in a darkened room by a flickering fire, a ghost story well told can still make the flesh creep better than anything on television.

Finally, everyone would gather round the piano and sing. They enjoyed special Christmas songs like *The Mistletoe Bough*, the tragic tale of a Christmas game of hide and seek. We also have to thank the Victorians for reviving the Christmas carol. At the beginning of Victoria's reign, carols were scarcely known in church, and the tradition of the 'waits', groups of singers going from door to door, was only kept up by a few seasonal mendicants. Many of the old carols were in danger of being forgotten, but the Victorians collected them and wrote many new ones,

> *In the bleak mid-winter*
> *Frosty wind made moan,*
> *Earth stood hard as iron,*
> *Water like a stone;*
> *Snow had fallen, snow on snow,*
> *Snow on snow,*
> *In the bleak mid-winter,*
> *Long ago.*

ABOVE: A rude awakening on Christmas Eve.

RIGHT: Carol singing with musical accompaniment.

FAR RIGHT: Attending the Christmas Eve service in perfect Christmas weather.

Never mind that in the land where Jesus was born the December temperature is in the eighties; this romantic picture of a frozen landscape perfectly encapsulates the Victorian image of the Christmas season.

Chapter Four

TRADITIONAL CHRISTMAS FARE

On Christmas day 1840 Queen Victoria with Prince Albert and seventeen guests sat down to Christmas dinner at Windsor Castle. They started with turtle soup, followed by a choice of haddock or sole, then roast beef or roast swan. For the fourth course there was veal, chicken, turbot, partridge or curried rabbit, followed by either pheasant or capon. Then came the mince pies, and a choice of eight sweets or savouries. A side table offered roast beef, roast mutton, roast turkey, a chine of pork, turkey pie (with larks and pheasants), partridge, brawn, sausages and boar's head.

Boar's head appeared on Victoria's side table, and continued to do so at Christmas dinner throughout her reign. This had been the centrepiece of the medieval Yuletide feast, but by Victorian times it was pretty hard to come by, and had generally been replaced by 'the roast beef of old England, a turkey, or a goose'. Alexis Soyer, the renowned chef of the Reform Club in mid-Victorian times produced a recipe for 'Pig's Head in Imitation of Wild Boar's Head', but more commonly in Victorian households, a pig's head would be turned into brawn, which was a great favourite.

While Victoria and her family were sitting down to dinner at Windsor Castle, even her humblest subjects were indulging in a special dinner of some kind. In *A Christmas Carol*, even before Scrooge had presented them with the prize turkey, Bob Crachit and his family were tucking into a veritable feast:

> *'There never was such a goose. Bob said he didn't believe there was ever such a goose cooked. Its tenderness and flavour, size and cheapness, were the themes of universal admiration. Eked out by the apple sauce and mashed potatoes, it was a sufficient dinner for the whole family; indeed, as Mrs. Crachit said with great delight (surveying one small atom of bone on the dish), they hadn't ate it all at last! Yet every one had had enough, and the youngest Crachits*

in particular were steeped in sage and onion to the eye-brows!'

Poor families like the Crachits would start saving with the 'Goose Club' in about September, paying in three-pence or sixpence a week, so that by the time Christmas came around they would have enough for a goose and

FAR LEFT: Bringing in the boar's head.

LEFT: Christmas shopping, by Harold Piffard.

BELOW: Carrying poultry to London on the Norwich stage coach.

perhaps a bottle of spirits. When Victoria came to the throne in 1837, goose was still the traditional Christmas dinner and large quantities of birds were imported from France and Germany, so that Leadenhall and Newgate markets would be packed with poultry the week before Christmas.

Turkey only appeared on the side table at Queen Victoria's 1840 Christmas dinner, but by the 1850s it had taken over from roast swan as the centrepiece of the royal repast, and was rapidly gaining popularity with ordinary families. The turkey was of course not native to Britain, but had been brought to Europe on one of Sebastian Cabot's ships on its return from the New World, where it had been hunted as a game bird in the wild woods of Alabama. Like geese, turkeys were imported into the London markets from the continent, but it wasn't long before turkey farming became established in Norfolk. The birds were driven up to London from August onwards, with little leather boots or a coating of tar on their feet to protect them during the long march. As the demand for Christmas turkeys increased however, they were slaughtered on the farm and sent up to London in December, as William Hervey recounts, by stagecoach:

> 'Many a time we have seen a Norfolk coach with its hampers piled on the roof and swung from beneath the body, and its birds depending, by every possible contrivance, from every part from which a bird could be made to hang. Nay, we believe it is not unusual with the proprietors, at this season, to refuse inside passengers of the human species in favour of these oriental gentry who "pay better".'

If middle-class households could not manage quite as many courses for Christmas dinner as the Queen, they

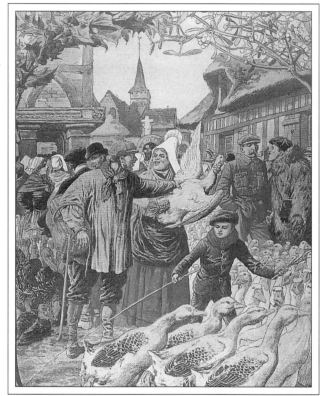

ABOVE: Selecting the most succulent Christmas bird.

RIGHT: Waylaid while delivering the Christmas dinner: an advertisement for Huntley & Palmers biscuits.

believed in having a jolly good try. The following Christmas menu, from the magazine *The Woman At Home* is costed at the princely sum of £1.13s.1d:

Celery Soup.
Cod a la Breme (garlic sauce).
Boned Quails.
Boiled Turkey. Mushroom Sauce.
Brussel Sprouts au Jus.
Roast Round of Beef.
Ox Tongue a la Belgravia.
Christmas Pudding. Wine Sauce.
Mince Pies. Orange Sponge Jelly

All the recipes for turkey in *The Woman At Home* recommend boiling it (in salted water with a carrot, some celery, an onion stuck with cloves and a bouquet garni), and serving it with a simple white sauce.

Turkey was boiled when it was to be followed by a rich joint of roast beef. But when it was the main dish of the feast, it was commonly presented roasted on a platter surrounded by savoury pork sausages, still linked together, which earned it the delightful sobriquet of 'Alderman In Chains'. Mrs Beeton in her *Book of Household Management* recommended that the bird be stuffed with forcemeat, but Eliza Acton in her splendid *Modern Cookery for Private Families* favoured chestnuts for both sauces and stuffings.

ABOVE: Stirring the Christmas pudding was an occasion in itself.

RIGHT: Presenting the pudding, aflame with brandy.

FAR RIGHT: Christmas Comes But Once A Year from Pears Christmas Annual, 1849.

To follow the turkey there was plum pudding, boiled in a muslin cloth in the copper (usually used for boiling the washing), which was why it came out the perfectly spherical shape we see in illustrations. Here are the Cratchit family in *A Christmas Carol*, having polished off their goose:

'Hallo! A great deal of steam! The pudding was out of the copper. A smell like a washing day! That was the cloth. A smell like a pastry cook's and an eating house next door to each other, with a laundress next door to that! That was the pudding. In half a minute, Mrs Crachit entered, flushed, but smiling proudly, with the pudding like a speckled cannon-ball, so hard and firm, blazing in half of half-a-quartern of ignited brandy, and bedight with Christmas holly stuck into the top.

Oh, a wonderful pudding! Bob Crachit said, and calmly too, that he regarded it as the greatest success achieved by Mrs Crachit since their marriage.'

The 'speckled cannon-ball' had its origins in something more liquid. Plum porridge was a kind of gruel, based on meat, or meat stock, laced with alcohol, thickened with breadcrumbs and sweetened with sugar and all sorts of dried fruit. It is not clear when plum porridge gave way to plum pudding, but by Victorian times the pudding was well established – although the plums which gave it its name (they were in fact prunes) had generally given way to imported currants and sultanas. Recipes abound, most of them very similar to those we use today, although Eliza Acton gives a special recipe for impoverished vegetarians, of which the principle ingredients are a pound of mashed potatoes and half a pound of carrots, beaten to a paste!

Mince pies too started out with meat as their number one ingredient; now only the suet remains. In earlier times the pies had been oval in shape, to represent the crib of the infant Jesus, and had even sometimes included a pastry baby on the top. Naturally when the Puritans banned Christmas in the seventeenth century, this was one of the first things to go. When mince pies were restored along with King Charles II, they tended on the whole to be round.

The baking of special cakes was associated with Twelfth Night rather than Christmas. It is said that

BELOW: *Queen Victoria's Twelfth cake, 1849.*

RIGHT: *Jellies, trifles and Christmas pudding, from Cassell's Household Guide.*

FAR RIGHT: *Santa Claus cake decoration, c.1900.*

Mary, Queen of Scots brought to her court from France the 'Feast of the Bean', in which a bean was baked into the cake and whoever found it was made 'king for the day'. Twelfth cakes were wonderful baroque edifices, more like modern wedding cakes; this was Queen Victoria's 1849 Twelfth cake, as described in *The Illustrated London News*:

> 'The cake was of regal dimensions, being about 30 inches in diameter, and tall in proportion: round the side the decorations consisted of strips of gilded paper, bowing outwards near the top, issuing from an elegant gold bordering. The figures, of which there were 16, on top of the cake, represented a party of the beaux and belles of the last century enjoying a repast al fresco *under some trees . . .'*

By the 1870s, however, Twelfth Night began to die out as a separate feast day, until it became simply the day when we take the decorations down. The special cake became a much more modest creation, to be eaten on Christmas day, although one major improvement was introduced: the practice of putting marzipan under the cake icing.

The Victorians collectively seem to have had a very sweet tooth, and confectioners did a roaring trade in toffee, fudge and nougat, chocolate nuts and marzipan fruits. But the particular reward for a virtuous child

1. Open Jelly with whipped cream.   2. Yorkshire Pie and Aspic Jelly.
3. Trifle, Ices and Jellies around.
4. Christmas Pudding.   5. Jelly of two colours.

sccms always to have been a sugar plum.

Sugar plums were a kind of crystallized fruit: plums that had been preserved since the autumn in syrup were given a crisp sugar coating. You can make them from reconstituted prunes, and other fruits (orange segments, apricots, whole grapes, even little apples) can be treated in exactly the same way.

'The fruits must be firm and not too ripe. Remove the skins, and cut any fruit containing stones in half and remove the stones, pare and remove stalks from small pears. Roll the fruit in caster sugar that contains a small spoonful each of cream of tartar and bicarbonate of soda to every pound. Pack separately on a dish and cover with sugar. Bake in a hot oven until fruit is tender; remove the dish, stand it in a cool larder, and before the fruit is set cold roll in the sugar mixture again and stand on a wire rack for twenty-four hours, then place in a box or tin with greaseproof paper between the layers.'

A box of candied fruit makes a delightful present, and as a finishing touch can be decorated with some crystallized mint leaves, made by coating the leaves with egg white, dusting them with caster sugar and drying in a slightly warm oven.

What did the Victorians have to drink at Christmas? The tradition of the 'wassail bowl' (a mixture of ale, sugar, nutmeg and roasted apples), while it continued in the countryside, was not quite the thing for the refined table. 'Bishop' was one of the most popular hot spiced wines in Victorian times, and here is Eliza Acton's 'Oxford Recipe for Bishop':

'Make several incisions in the rind of a lemon, stick cloves in these, and roast the lemon by a slow fire. Put small but equal quantities of cinnamon, cloves, mace and allspice with a trace of ginger, into a saucepan with half a pint of water: let it boil until it is reduced by one half. Boil one bottle of port wine, burn a portion of the spirit out of it by applying a lighted paper to the saucepan; put the roasted lemon and spice into the wine; stir it up well and let it stand

*near the fire ten minutes. Rub a few knobs of sugar
on the rind of the lemon, put the sugar into a bowl or
jug, with the juice of half a lemon (not roasted), pour
the wine into it, grate in some nutmeg, sweeten it to
the taste, and serve it up with the lemon and spice
floating in it.'*

This sounds like a recklessly extravagant use of port.
Cheap red wine, heated but not boiled, can be used to
equally good effect, since the sugar, spice and lemon
will mask any roughness. *Cassell's Family Magazine*,
however, is not in favour of cheap wine; here it is
wrestling with the problem of what to give children to
drink for a party:

*'Plain water is decidedly best. Champagne is
expensive and unnecessary. Port wine negus is very
nice, but not exactly suitable with meat. Many
children will drink water, or a little sherry and water;
but for moderately sized children, who do not care to
take water, what can be better than home-made
lemonade? To my thinking a glass of lemonade is far
preferable to cheap champagne, and far less vulgar.
Why poison your guests for the sake of appearances?'*

*FAR LEFT: Candied fruits and
fudges make lovely gifts when
attractively presented.*

*LEFT: A German family await
their Christmas dinner with
unmasked enthusiasm.*

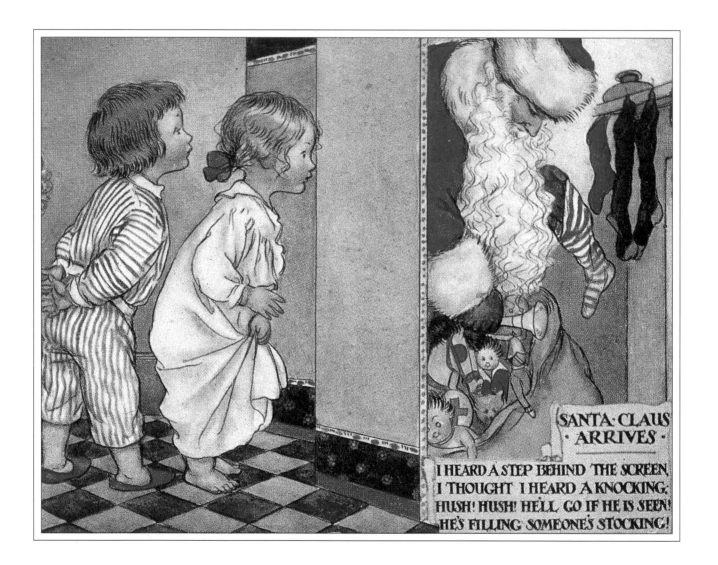

SANTA·CLAUS
·ARRIVES

I HEARD A STEP BEHIND THE SCREEN,
I THOUGHT I HEARD A KNOCKING,
HUSH! HUSH! HE'LL GO IF HE IS SEEN!
HE'S FILLING SOMEONE'S STOCKING!

Chapter Five

THE SPIRIT
OF GIVING

Christmas would not be Christmas if there was no Santa Claus. Nor would it be the same if we did not send and receive cards, and give presents to our families and friends. But these traditions only developed during the reign of Queen Victoria. The giving of presents had been a New Year custom, but even that was in decline. Christmas boxes (seasonal donations to the poor and to the servants) were commonplace, however, and in *Sketches by Boz* Dickens suggests that when grandmama was buying treats for the servants, she would buy them for the children as well.

*ABOVE: Returning from a
Christmas shopping expedition.*

*RIGHT: Some useful gift ideas
from The Lady, 1896.*

*FAR RIGHT: A Christmas
Morning Visit, 1896.*

But when we come to *A Christmas Carol*, present-giving seems to be the order of the day. The Spirit of Christmas Past takes Scrooge to see the family of the girl he might have married, just as father returns home:

> *. . . attended by a man laden with Christmas toys and
> presents. Then the shouting and the struggling, and
> the onslaught that was made on the defenceless porter!
> The scaling him with chairs for ladders to dive into
> his pockets, despoil him of brown-paper parcels, hold
> on tight by his cravat, hug him round his neck,
> pommel his back, and kick his legs in irrepressible
> affection! The shouts of wonder and delight with
> which the development of every package was
> received!*

As with the Christmas tree, Prince Albert may well have had a hand in popularizing the custom of present-giving; his biography says that the Prince thought Christmas day was 'a day for the exchange of presents, as marks of mutual affection and good-will'. But when *Punch* wrote about Christmas shopping in 1849, it was to describe the grocers, confectioners, poulterers and other purveyors of Christmas fare, not presents. As the century progressed however the gift industry mushroomed, until by 1887 one trader was offering no less than a hundred thousand gift ideas, and magazines were full of advertisements and articles on the subject. *Lady's*

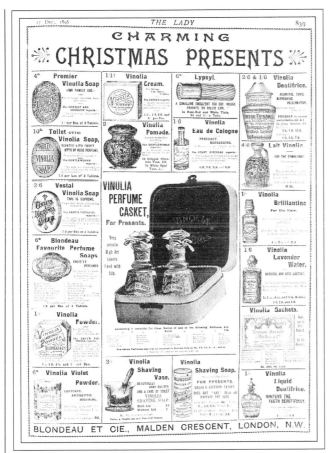

these days, any more than we can live without a 'dangle' of sorts. Some of the most delightful of these latter are the little diamond lucky pigs, with ruby eyes and curly tails, frogs in diamonds and emeralds, stars and trefoils.

Or if diamonds were not the thing, how about 'Whiffs from the South of France'? Particularly recommended

Realm particularly recommends 'Yuletide Novelties from the Parisian Diamond Company':

    . . . *we cannot exist without a Louis XVI buckle*

as a suitable gift for a man is H.P. Truefitt's Lavender Water, because 'it is recognized that the one scent a man is not ashamed to use is Lavender'.

But as the festive season centred so much on children, it was, then as now, toys which were most heavily marketed. For girls there were dolls, such as Miss Dolly Daisie Dimple, the Barbie doll of her day, advertised as 'the Craze of the Season', who came with a trunk full of clothing, all for the princely sum of one shilling. And then there were the dolls' houses, perfect in every detail of decor and furnishing. For boys there were trains, boats and carriages, often the most exquisite working models, and toy soldiers. Then there were games;

LEFT: *A little girl dreams of Christmas morning.*

ABOVE: *Another Christmas Eve dream, in which the toys come alive.*

RIGHT: *The delights of Christmas Morning, by Charles Robinson.*

Snakes and Ladders, Happy Families, Draughts, Ludo were all around in Victoria's day.

But of course presents didn't need to be extravagant and expensive. The delightfully named A.A. Strange Butson writing in the children's magazine *Little Folks* maintains that 'nearly everyone values more a gift that has been specially made for them than the smartest bought thing'. The expectation was clearly that little girls were very deft with their needles, and could turn their hand to embroidered aprons, or 'a warm quilted cape of some dark silk edged with fur' for grandmama. Boys meanwhile were expected to be a dab hand at fretwork, making for papa a writing case or for mama ornamental picture frames.

Some of the suggestions still have practical value. A jar of home-made jam or chutney, complete with hand-painted label, can be topped with a cover made from a circle of fabric, edged with lace. Lavender bags, for sweet scented drawers, can be made from scraps of fabric and ribbon, stuffed with dried lavender. A more powerful air freshener is a pomander, made by sticking cloves into an orange, and then rolling it in a mixture of cinnamon, nutmeg, allspice and orris-root. Tie a ribbon around it so that it can be hung in a wardrobe or airing cupboard.

It was during the Victorian era that Christmas cards

CHRISTMAS MORNING

came into their own. Previously, people had exchanged Christmas greetings by letter, and schoolchildren often prepared Christmas Pieces for their parents or grandparents, a kind of sampler of their best handwriting on special paper with a printed border.

RIGHT: *Summer scenes were not unusual among the first Christmas cards.*

BELOW: *The first Christmas card, commissioned by Henry Cole in 1843.*

FAR RIGHT: *A Christmas card of the 1850s, clearly influenced by the Valentine.*

in its central panel, a jolly family sitting down to their Christmas dinner, and raising their glasses in a toast, while two smaller side panels portrayed acts of seasonal charity, feeding the hungry and clothing the naked. In 1846 a thousand copies of this design were printed and sold for a shilling a copy.

The idea didn't really catch on however, and it was not until the 1860s that printers recognized a potential business opportunity and started manufacturing cards in bulk. These early cards were like postcards, not folded as they are today, and the trade was given a boost in 1870 by the introduction of the halfpenny post for cards or unsealed envelopes.

In the late decades of the century the practice of sending cards became so widespread that the Post Office had difficulty coping with the seasonal mail. A correspondent to *The Times* after the Christmas rush of 1877 described the sending of Christmas cards as a 'social evil', and complained at 'the delay of legitimate correspondence by cartloads of children's cards'. But in 1883 *The Times* concluded:

This wholesome custom has been . . . frequently the happy means of ending strifes, cementing broken friendships and strengthening family and neighbourhood ties in all conditions of life. In this respect the Christmas card undoubtedly fulfils a high

The Valentine card had been around for some time, so it is quite surprising that it took the Christmas card so long to get off the ground. It is generally thought that the person responsible for the first Christmas card was Henry Cole, director of the newly-founded Victoria and Albert Museum. In 1843 he commissioned H.C. Horsley, R.A. to produce a suitable design. It depicted,

Merry Christmas Greeting.
At this glad time our thoughts will stray,
To loved ones far away,
And we wish them all prosperity
And a happy Christmas Day!

tine cards than Christmas cards, for the simple reason that the manufacturers already produced Valentines and it was easy to use the same card and just change the greeting. So Christmas greetings were conveyed with cupids, bows, lace edging, and as with most things Victorian, flowers everywhere. Pretty soon however, Christmassy themes began to predominate, with the traditional scenes of snow-laden landscapes, holly and mistletoe, Christmas trees and bells, Father Christmas, plum puddings and robins. There is a legend that robins got their red breasts by fanning with their wings the fire that was warming the baby Jesus, and scorched themselves, hence their association with Christmas.

end, for cheap postage has constituted it almost exclusively the modern method of conveying Christmas wishes, and the increasing popularity of the custom is for this reason, if no other, a matter for congratulation.'
Early mass-produced cards were often more like Valen-

As swiftly wings the time away,
We give again to Christmas day
A HEARTY WELCOME!

It is surprising how few Christmas cards had religious themes, because piety was an important element in the Victorian Christmas. An astonishing number had nothing to do with Christmas whatever; there were summer flowers, dogs and cats, horses and cows, even a famous series of nudes at the seaside! H. Gleeson White, who in 1894 published a lengthy study on the subject of Christmas cards commented on the incongruity of much of the subject matter, and deplored:

. . . tragic sunsets, haunted churchyards, consumptive choirboys, monsters of might-make land, pictures of accidents dear to the farce writer, and, in short, the subjects which are in vulgar parlance "weird" and alarming on the one hand, and distinctly uncomfortable on the other.

The humour in comic cards was often pretty crude, and likely to offend if sent to the wrong person. 'I am a poor man', writes Mr Pooter in *The Diary Of A Nobody* 'but I would gladly give ten shillings to find out who sent me the insulting Christmas card I received this morning.' Poor old Pooter never could take a joke.

Santa Claus was quite unknown before Victorian times, although 'Old Father Christmas', 'Sir Christmas', even plain 'Mr Christmas' had been a symbol of the season for centuries, popping up in mummers' plays, medieval carols and Elizabethan masques. He is said to be based on St Nicholas, who had been a bishop noted for his benevolence in fourth century Asia Minor, but his origins go back even further. St Nicholas was co-opted in by the Church to give Christian respectability to the old pagan custom of mid-winter present giving. After the Protestant Reformation in Europe however, the worship of saints was frowned upon, and veneration of St Nicholas's saintly qualities was replaced by an emphasis on merry twinkling joviality.

The tradition of hanging up stockings definitely owes its origin to St Nicholas, who was reputed to be

CHRISTMAS

Little Robin-Redbreast
To the window comes,
Seeking warmth and shelter,
Asking us for crumbs.
Shall we not remember
All outside our door,
Whom the chill December
Finds hungry, sad, and poor?

A Happy Christmas.

FAR LEFT: *Robins were a favourite subject for Christmas cards.*

LEFT: *A romantic walk in the snow, from a Victorian postcard.*

BELOW: *Hanging up stockings by the fireplace.*

enormously rich, and much given to distributing largesse among the deserving poor. One recipient found a bag of gold in a stocking she had hung up to dry in front of the fire; St Nicholas had evidently thrown it down the chimney.

In the early nineteenth century the bringer of gifts and good cheer was usually known as 'the Spirit of Christmas', and was portrayed as a rather bacchanalian old chap with a glass in his hand. Even in the 1860s and 70s, Christmas card designers couldn't agree about his appearance: sometimes he had a beard, sometimes he didn't, and he wore a variety of clothing, by no means

ABOVE: An early Victorian incarnation of Father Christmas.

RIGHT: Father Christmas in what became his traditional garb.

FAR RIGHT: A pair of jolly Santas from the 1900s.

always red, though he usually had a jaunty garland of holly in his hair.

It was in fact the Americans who created the standard image, and gave him the alternative name Santa Claus (from the Dutch-American name for St Nicholas). The illustrator Thomas Nast came up with the definitive physical image in his drawings for *Harper's Weekly*: the flowing beard, the portly figure in a red suit and cap – though British artists generally preferred an enveloping robe to the furry coat and trousers that Nast depicts.

By far the most enduring image of Father Christmas/ Santa Claus comes from Clement Clark Moore's 1822 poem *A Visit from St Nicholas*. 'Twas the night before Christmas', it begins, and goes on to describe the arrival of St Nicholas at the sleeping house;

> *He was dressed all in fur from his head to his foot,*
> *And his clothes were all tarnished with ashes and soot;*
> *A bundle of toys he had flung on his back,*
> *And he looked like a pedlar just opening his pack.*
> *His eyes how they twinkled! his dimples how merry!*
> *His cheeks were like roses, his nose like a cherry;*
> *His droll little mouth was drawn up in a bow,*
> *And the beard on his chin was as white as the snow.*
> *The stump of a pipe he held tight in his teeth,*
> *And the smoke it encircled his head like a wreath.*
> *He had a broad face, and a little round belly*

That shook, when he laughed, like a bowl full of jelly.
He was chubby and plump, – a right jolly old elf –
And I laughed when I saw him, in spite of myself.

Quite a transformation from the ascetic bishop of fourth century Asia Minor! Why did this American immigrant who arrived in a sleigh drawn by those outlandish creatures, reindeer, take over so completely from the Christmas characters of the European tradition, like Old Mr Christmas and the Christkind? Because he embodied everything that the Victorians wanted to celebrate. Jovial, convivial and full of laughter, kindly, generous and philanthropic children were the centre of his world. In fact he was the very epitome of the Victorian spirit of Christmas.

Acknowledgements

Bridgeman Art Library: Front cover; 6a; 14a; 18a; 20a; 48a; 66a; 69b. Hulton Deutsch Collection: 8a; 9b; 16a; 17b; 31b; 46a; 47c; 51c; 55b; 62a; 64b. Christmas Archives: 10a; 17c; 21c; 22a; 23b; 29b; 31c; 32b; 34b; 35c; 47b; 57c; 67c; 70a; 71c. Mary Evans: 10b; 11c; 27b; 27c; 28a; 30a; 32a; 34a; 39c; 40a; 41b; 43b; 50a; 52a; 53b; 54a; 57b; 59b; 63c; 67b; 68a. Punch Library: 12a; 44a. Fine Art Photographic Library: 12b; 13c; 24a; 26a; 29c; 36a; 38a; 45b; 45c; 51b; 55c; 60a; 64a; 65c; 69c; 71b. Illustrated London News: 19b; 20b; 41c; 56a. The Dickens Museum: 42a. The British Museum: 63b. Octopus Library: 23c; 33c; 58a.